Déjà Vu

poems by

Laura L. Hansen

Finishing Line Press
Georgetown, Kentucky

Déjà Vu

Copyright © 2017 by Laura L. Hansen
ISBN 978-1-63534-278-9 First Edition
All rights reserved under International and Pan-American Copyright Conventions.
No part of this book may be reproduced in any manner whatsoever without written permission from the publisher, except in the case of brief quotations embodied in critical articles and reviews.

ACKNOWLEDGMENTS

These are the Places We Encountered Each Other won First Place for Poetry in the 2016 Brainerd Writers Alliance Writing Contest
The Foragers first appeared in Martin Lake Poetry Workshop, Selected Poems, 2016, Hucklenut Press, St. Paul, MN
Strange and Beautiful Gifts was featured in the online blog, Ever Ready, in February 2016
Her Body was included in the Crossing Arts Alliance Exhibit, Dimensions of Motherhood, 2016
Cupping Stones and *Undressing the World* were selected for the Crossing Arts Alliance 2015 Poetry on the Wall Exhibit
The Love Game aired on Northland Public Radio's "The Beat"
Wearing Mother's Genes was awarded Frist Place in the League of Minnesota Poets 2016 Blizzard Writers Award Category
Sensible Shoes appeared in a slightly different form under the title *Portrait of Mother at 83* in the Crossing Arts Alliance Dimensions of Motherhood Exhibit, 2016

Publisher: Leah Maines

Editor: Christen Kincaid

Cover Art: Laura L. Hansen, Photo by Christina Johnson Photography

Author Photo: Christina Johnson Photography

Cover Design: Elizabeth Maines McCleavy

Printed in the USA on acid-free paper.
Order online: www.finishinglinepress.com
          www.indiebound.org
          also available on amazon.com

                    Author inquiries and mail orders:
                          Finishing Line Press
                              P. O. Box 1626
                        Georgetown, Kentucky 40324
                                  U. S. A.

Table of Contents

Déjà vu 1
These Are the Places We Encountered Each Other 2
The Truth Upon Waking 3
The Heartbreak of Birds 4
Laissez-Faire 5
The Foragers 6
The Lector of the Hive 7
The Gifts They Bring 8
Strange and Beautiful Gifts 9
The Thing about Live Music 10
Her Body 11
What She Carries Beneath the Skin 12
Cupping Stones 13
The Love Game 14
The Blue Pill 15
Wearing Mother's Genes 16
Sensible Shoes 17
Undressing the World 18
After the Storms 19
Barbarians at the Gate 20
Testimony 21
Children Behave 22
Hymnal 23
Why Women Go Running in the Woods Alone Against
    All Rational Advice 24
The Mythology of Loneliness 25
The Logic of the Heart 26
The Call in the Night 27
When the World Burns from the Top Down 28
Two Herons and a Blood Red Moon 29
A Cup of Sky 30
What Poets Do 31
I've Lost the Language 32
Sometimes I Pray that You Won't Talk to Me 33
Surely It Hasn't Come to This 34
Mitosis 35
Desire, At Sixty 36

Déjà vu 1:04 AM

That star flickering to the west
is neither firefly nor star
but a plane fardistant.
Its light stitches tiny openings
in the nearnight sky
like an uneven seam.
I wait for a hidden hand
to tear along the perforated
line, to allow the moon
to drop below its dark curtain.
Every time I write this
I think I have written it
before, like a string once
pulled, how it just keeps
unraveling.

These are the Places We Encountered Each Other

At the screen door listening to cicadas.
In the metallic silence after storms.
At first light, at the music store,
in the cemetery after snow.
In the long season before summer.
After a movie, in the rain.

We shared a cup of sky before bed,
paddled our way halfway to the moon,
portaged our Duluth pack, our dried food,
our back packs and paddles
all up and down the river.
You read LeCarre and I, Thoreau.

The Truth upon Waking

This morning I dreamt that an otter and a wolf, both sleek
and black, were lying down in the driveway of the gas station.

I gathered my shopping bags, contents tumbled and hastily
repackaged, from the ground and made to walk past.

The wolf rose, tail high, and stepped forward to block my way.
He lowered his shoulders like an all-star tackle, sunlight sharp

in his see-all eyes. I waited. He paused, turned, circled once
and sat down again as if I had nothing he wanted.

I heaved my parcels higher and slipped by the resting pair,
ember-eyed wolf, oil-slick otter, as they nudged each other.

Whatever it was they were to each other, whatever it was
I seemed to them (there in that most unlikely of places),

I knew that it was I with my silly burden and busy hands,
strangled by the handles of my plastic bags, that was

not really there—an empty container, wasting air.

The Heartbreak of Birds

We hear the thud on the plate glass window, find them—
nothing more than twisted feathers and rapid breath—
    below the window,
        laid out on the grass.

What is it they want in here that they don't already have?
The fringe of the throw for a nest?
    The mirrored-face in the fresh-
        washed window for a mate?

Birds have trees—wispy locusts, burly oaks, graceful
willows, stately elms. Birds, those rusty robins
    and cherry red cardinals,
        have sky—endlessly blue.

Birds—have homes that rest in the curve of the ash,
in the deepest hedge. Birds have lift, and loft, and down,
    have iridescence, have
        borderless lives.

What do I have in here that they could possibly want?
What is it they want that they don't already have?
    If I jumped through the glass
        I still couldn't fly.

Laissez-Faire
> *a policy or attitude of letting things take their own course,*
> *without interfering*

Let the grass grow until it swallows the deck,
let it go to seed until the deck boards
are covered in grains as if swept by sand.

Let the grass grow, let lilies of the valley
bleed into the untamed grass, each tiny
white-blood drop a memory that will vanish

soon enough, or live on—a pearl as strong
as a tiny hurt that waits beneath the skin,
beneath the sand, beneath the seed

on the deck and the grass and my restless
feet that move and move and move
like the thick-growing wind-blown grass.

The Foragers

In Ohio, the drywallers took a break,
walked the untilled humus-soft hillside,
and found the morels, helped themselves
picking under and around the rotten
stump until all traces of mushroom
were gone.

Later that summer, we rambled
down the hill, tripping over vines
and deadfall, tangled our sleeves
in the cobweb of underbrush,
until we came to the old home-made
dam of concrete block and rock.

The blackberries, wild, their leaves
minty green, were rushing over
the dried-up spillway, dashing
from stump to block to stone.
We pushed back our sleeves
and picked and picked.

The next year the morels
were gone, over-picked,
but the flood of blackberries
came on strong. Disturbed
or undisturbed, they owned
that corner of the yard, ruled
the one-and-a-quarter acre
that we had mistaken
for our own.

The Lector of the Hive

Speak
for the honeycomb,
for the soft waxy
understructure
tasteless but filled,
encased, dripping
with sweet honey,
loved intensely
by the sugared tongues
of bees.

Speak
for the long tubular
bells of flowers
who suffer the abrupt
invasion
of the sugar seekers—
the hummingbirds,
the honeybees.

Speak
for those
whose pale bodies
store
and for those
whose flamboyance
requires them
to give
and to give and to give.

The sugar is the thing,
the proboscis
that excavates,
the bees that bear down
on flower after flower
with pollen on their feet—
matchmaking, reforesting.

The Gifts They Bring

One brings me stones, a few agates,
beautiful in their imperfection.
It is like a message, to be okay,
to accept.

Another brings me bits of wood,
rough-edged or beaver-smoothed,
it doesn't matter…they are all
of the same family—tree.

Yet another gifted me
with a rabbit, a black Netherland
Dwarf that led to two more
of equal but different perfection.

And then there was the friend that gifted
me with a lifetime subscription
to the New Yorker on the condition
I tried to help him understand the poems.

And then there is you, with your thousand-
piece puzzles and uncomplicated demands:
eat less salt, let me read that book
when you have finished with it.

These are my gifts, my friends,
that I have been given but do not deserve.
They accumulate like leaves
brought in

by a surprise gust of wind
but only a few remain, stuck to the
dew-wet grass, picked up for a certain
shape or hue and pressed here

between the pages of my book.
They are worn, familiar, mismatched.
They have absorbed the sun, the rain,
fed upon good earth, flown on the wind.

Strange and Beautiful Gifts

The sky howled down
and threw out its lightning fists
and struck the tree
at its crown.

Limbs were severed;
the tree was seared at its core.
Bark exploded into shards
and fell to the ground
like a maelstrom of javelins.

Weeks later she collected them;
cradled them in her arms
as if they were the last
harvest of the season.
She brought them inside
the little cabin
and tended to them.

Now as winter sets it eyes
on the ragged ground
where the tree once stood
she begins to visit neighbors
and friends, gifting them
with small bundles
of the dried and shaggy bark.

It is all she can do
to extend the life of what was taken,
trusting those who receive
to spread the ashes, to make of them
their own creation.

The Thing about Live Music
Lehto and Wright at Great River Arts, March 4, 2016

Music explodes off stringed guitars,
marches across the table.

Notes ping up arms, into chest,
snap and sizzle like an electrical charge.

>We live the songs. Our bodies
>expel rhythm, breathe melody.

A quick upstroke across the twelve string
snaps our heads back, a sudden twang…

then a smooth chord progression
softens our shoulders.

>The musicians are playing
>the instrument of our bodies.

The sound of the Bodhran is so real,
so organic, we don't know

if what we feel is the drum beating
or the beating of our own hearts.

>Soon, the show over, deft hands
>will lay us down, shut our bodies

away in shapely felt-lined cases
where we will wait, like the guitar

and the mandolin, for the hands of the
musicians to bring us life again.

Her Body

At the edge of her body are nerves,
raw and exposed, that chafe
at the touch of the wind,
the rub of her clothes.

At the edge of her body
are little ganglia of thought,
ones she's allowed to escape
but were better left unsaid.

At the center of her body
is a hard knot of fear,
a sadness that bleeds.
All of her interior life

lives on a raft that drifts
the length of her midriff,
a sea that churns and shifts,
ebbs and pulls.

At the edge of her body are places
she's never explored, small bits of flesh
that saunter off the edge
and plunge into the cluttered air.

What She Carries Beneath the Skin

She clenches the sliver of almond between her teeth
sucks hard
looking for the familiar extract
the cherry red scent
she associates with her mother's
almond cake
but the nut is hard
and gives up nothing
so small and slender
and pale
foods rarely give up what they are
so easily
the grain must be threshed
the cream churned
the pepper ground
she is quicker to give up her essence
she exhales and the air is whorled
scented with blossom
yellow with the forsythia burst of spring
she bites down hard, she breathes, she blooms.

Cupping Stones

Cupping hands over ears, I hear the sea thrumming
as if holding a whelk to myself, a rushing deep and low
connects me to the water's surge and ebb, to my own
inner ebb and flow.

From inside my self-made cocoon of flesh and bone,
pulse and blood, I gather thoughts like stones,
holding them pensively, rattling them in my palms.
I gently discard the ones that are too flashy, too

bold, and save for myself the little river stones,
the ones that are flannel gray and smooth, soothing
to the touch. This is where I will live now, I tell
myself. This is home.

The Love Game

She pedals her fingers
around the tips
of the daisies—

feels each petal as it ravishes
her fingertips. She twirls
the sticky green stems

until they spin
like a carousel.
Her breath gallops

at the sight of their slight universes
spinning
on the axis of her will.

The Blue Pill

You know the one, the blue pill that is tiny as a seed, that slips
through your fingers and bounces off the laminate countertop

making a sound like a dog's toenails on hardwood floors.
It tip-taps twice then skitters under the vanity cupboard

as shy and quick as a mouse. The blue pill has slipped away.
All its promise of sunny skies and happy thoughts is now hidden

in the far-dark corner of the bathroom, all that bright-eyed optimism
lies tangled up in dog hair and dust, just out of reach though you go

to hands and knees, reach with crabbed arthritic fingers, sneeze.
The little blue pill of your heart isn't even laughing at you,

just lies in wait, useless, almost invisible. You rise and try
the child-proof cap again, aggravated and alone.

You squeeze your fingers tighter together this time,
try to cup that too-small bit of blue in your hand,

turn the water on, lift the chipped pink cup, slowly
open your palm as if to release a captured firefly.

Wearing Mother's Genes

All day today I will look like my mother,
brown eyes the color of coffee
looking critically
at the messy house.
I will think like my mother, see
like my mother,
as I shuffle jars around in the fridge
trying to restore things to her
idea of order.

All day today I will look like my mother,
capacious hips stretching thin
the blue cotton of the slacks
I wear most days.
I will move about
on the same stout legs,
heavy thighs rubbing
like the pulse of a train
chuff-chuff-chuffing.

All day I will try to keep
from tucking my hair behind my ears,
avoid the semblance of mother's
preferred pixie-cut style.
I will avoid mirrors and reflective
plate-glass windows but she will be there
walking beside me, within me,
present. All day.

Sensible Shoes

Mother, after the stroke, is like a pillow
that constantly needs fluffing, won't hold
its shape, her turtlenecks twist

and sag, her arms dangle, her feet
stray at odd angles never quite resting
on the wheelchair's supportive steel plates.

I remember her feet, swollen, after
bunion surgery, darkly stitched
and the long rows of high heels in her closet.

Mother often told me you have to suffer
to be beautiful, but she should have
warned her toes instead.

Before the stroke, Mother was like
a straight-backed chair, upright, rigid,
unforgiving. Now her shoulders slope

and her head drops forward as if in apology,
but when she raises her head to meet my gaze
her eyes lock with mine and I know

she forgives nothing. I get up and give her
a stiff hug, willing it to be soft,
meaningful, and as I turn to leave

I hear my sensible rubber-soled shoes
squeak, squeak, squeak
down the long linoleum-tiled hall.

Undressing the World

The back yard is slowly undressing itself.
First to go was the willow tree
and her lacy chartreuse leaves
that the yard wore long and loose.
It fell one quiet summer day—
just slipped to the side
and lay in the grass
in a tangle of its own soft tresses.
Next was the northernmost elm—
the one that shouldered up
to the neighbor's yard
and protected us like a greatcoat
from river-borne winter winds.
The hedgerows
along the granite walls
that hemmed the yard
like decorative piping
disassembled over the years
and the yard just cast them aside
leaving us to dig
the last of the brittle roots.
Now the ash are dying
and one by one we pull them down
like last season's dresses, three last fall
and today the straight-line wind
and hail has pared the last one
away, pulling down limbs
like torn-at-the-seam sleeves.
The yard shows a little more flesh
each year, and even the lawn
is aging. The yard is uneven
and more weed than grass—
dimpled and wrinkled as
an old woman's skin.
That is why we plant new trees—
maple saplings and river birch.
We watch the stump of the willow
stretch new suckers toward the sun
and believe in the blessing of undressing.

After the Storms

The chrysanthemums—shorn
from their stems by wind—were blown up into the sky
where they danced with the stars
until morning arrived
washing them down
to the earth
where their stalks lay
like downed trees
and they could not attach themselves again
so shriveled there on the ground to mothwing dust,
but oh the night of playing with the stars,
wafting on the wind, that
was the thing.

Barbarians at the Gate

Slam-slam-slam, the wind punches the window
in a volley of gusts, a fist fight breaks out
among the trees, angry arms flailing.

Slam—the lawn chairs somersault over
the patio fence, tumble like drunkards
into the neighbor's yard.

The world is angry tonight.

Whump. Whump. The shutters fling
themselves against the metal siding, bruised
and bruising the defenseless house.

Rain gutters down, slaps grass—
angry as that father down the street,
the one that sent his wife to hospital last week.

The weather is wicked tonight.

Lightning cracks open the skull of sky,
tattoos the elm to its root.
Children stumble wide-eyed from bed.

Again, the sky issues a hammer-crack,
a tree splits open in the dark.
Waves pile up on the shore
willing their way into the yard,
willing their way up to the house.
We will not sleep tonight.

We will not sleep tonight.

Testimony

Was he shaking when he put the barrel of the handgun
to chin and aimed it up into cranium? Was he
leaning in to get the angle right? Was he close enough
to see the soft blonde hairs that framed her 18-year-old lips?

Or was his hand steady, the trained hand of a long-time
security officer, at ease with guns?
Was he smiling as he sat in the chair at the foot
of the stairs and waited for her to come down?

First her booted feet, next her denim-clad ankles,
a shin, a knee, a thigh, her hips, then shoot.
How much of her did he need to see to know
that he wanted her dead? How many minutes

after shooting the boy did he wait for her?
He must have paced through the night,
their bodies bleeding out, turning to brown
rust on the basement floor.

How does one sleep with those two teen bodies
stiffening in the workroom? How polite of him
not to bother the police on a holiday, how horrific
to state so unemotionally that he

put her out of her misery, a good clean—
clean, mind you—killing shot, as if he was filling out
his doe permit, as if he were putting meat by
for the long lonely winter.

Children Behave
I Think We're Alone Now by Tommy James and the Shondells

Like a child writing with invisible ink,
I run my river-wetted finger
along the granite wall
creating each letter of your name
from nothing more than rock
and sun and heat and flesh
and water. Five letters,

five essential ingredients.
I write it in the sand of beaches
I've never seen. I scrawl it in dust
on the cluttered coffee table.
I pen it on the mud-streaked rear windows
of strangers' cars in big anonymous
parking lots.

When we were teens, before
we started the awkward dance,
I wrote your name
on the sides of my bumper shoes
in blue Bic ink. I wrote it
on the inside of my desk drawer
with the names of other boys

I thought were keen.
Later, I wrote your name
with my tongue across your
pale neck. Nothing is left
of that kiss but a memory
of sweet salt and the aftertaste
of wet granite.

Hymnal

She loves the duplicity of the night,
the expansiveness that makes her feel
like she could walk forever, walk into
    the long shadows
thrown by the streetlights into another life.

She loves the tight circle the saturated air
forms around her as she moves, hugging her
like a sable jacket, a bullet-proof vest.
In the nighttime she is fluid, her
    innate clumsiness

    left behind.
On the darkly-pebbled tarmac
her arms extend into dance, her feet move
to her own rhythms, jazz, rock,
sentimental ballads, Lutheran hymns.

These days when she stays in at night
her legs keep walking.
They scissor back and forth
    under sheets
the color of spring trees.

They wake her with their jerk and stomp.
Better, she decides, to go out walking
hand in hand with the moon
under the staccato stars than to pace
the length of the bed each night.

And so she goes out walking,
a citizen
    of the long-
        shadowed night.

Why Women Go Running in the Woods Alone Against All Rational Advice

Once she walked an alpine trail
and woke a sleeping moose

that rose from the sunless path
like a slow-moving bear

leaving her small and breathless
and suddenly unsure

of her wild and reckless
nature.

Once she swam in a mirthless river
until she was shivering

and bone-cold blue.
She rose from the shivering water

and pulled herself ashore
on wobbly rubbery legs

and was suddenly aware
of her wild and confident

strength.

The Mythology of Loneliness

The house
with its permeable bricks
and crumbling windowsills

appeared
reflected in the water,
everything paired with itself,

the trees divested of leaves
fine in their dark sketchery,
the weathered shed.

But where was the red boat
that would bring her back to the shore,
that would deliver her back to herself?

How lucky the squirrel, she thought,
to clatter from tree to tree,
to feel the leaves

pass over his shoulders
like healing hands,
to see

in each knothole
and from the farthest reach of branch
the sun leading the way home.

The Logic of the Heart

As deeply as a diamond cutting glass,
the words slice into her, part her.
She is left neither shattered nor whole.
He rolls the beguiling bauble over his tongue,
clenches it between teeth, taunts.
But never again will her left-brain
be troubled by the aching desires of the right.
Never again the deep cut, never again
the hard slap of separation.
She is, has been, riven.
She looks at her mirror images,
one still in the frame, the other askew,
and knows what can never be made whole.
She lets her open wound stain the broken glass
and a new beauty is revealed.
Inside the cathedral of her heart
the vaulted nave is split by the long roof beam
and all the clerestory windows leak red light.
As deeply as a diamond cutting glass,
she loves her life.

The Call in the Night

It is the oldest story in the world;
child claws its way out of the womb,
eats you out of house and home,
demands the keys to the car then crashes
on a sharp curve under a spring moon,
the wild horse of his grandfather
galloping away from the farm,
the proud ghost of his father
signed up and marching
off to war. The oldest
story in the world, the knock
on the door, the women—
mothers, girlfriends, wives—
white-knuckled and waiting.
A young girl bangs on my
midnight door, a streak of blood
across cheek, behind her
a young man with jean jacket
blotting the split-open wound
on his head, the car just down the hill
merged to tree. *Please open the door,
but don't call the police.*
Their frightened faces quieting even
the dog. Hand over glass of water,
close enough to drink the fumes.
Liquor, blood, young love, defiance,
fear. It is the oldest story in the world.

When the World Burns from the Top Down

When the world burns from the top down,
from the snowless Alaskan tundra
to the parched Canadian prairie

the sun in Minnesota glows muddled orange
like a sodium streetlamp that fails to turn off
on a foggy morning. When wildfires burn

for days and weeks in the north, the ashy
grey haze sinks slowly south, slips past
border crossings and customs check points,

infiltrates the northern states until
the mornings dawn like dirty dishwater.
In this half-light holiday, the fireworks

seem a cruel irony, fire begets smoke
and smoke gobbles up any sight of
the fire-popping array.

In the mottled gray end-of-day sky,
we sense a sun we cannot see
setting.

Two Herons and a Blood Red Moon

Tonight, two great blue herons down by the lake
and a blood red moon. No photos.
You'll just have to imagine them there
improbably balanced on chopstick-thin legs
like a pair of yoga practitioners—
one foot rooted to the ground,
the other bent at the knee, suspended.
Go further, imagine yourself there
waiting in the reeds, attuned to the touch
of lithe and twisting fish who curve slowly past
in the shallow water drinking in the last warm afternoon light.
Sink gently down, letting your head—heavy, heavy—lead you.
Let your arms drape down like the branches of the willow.
Become the water, the friend of the heron,
the sustainer. Become a container, a bowl
to hold reflected light—sun, moon, full moon,
waning moon, red.

A Cup of Sky

Cupped, her hands
are like a slotted spoon,
the cold tap water meant
for washing the long gray day away
slipping through
and singing false promises
down the drain.

Will it be the same
if she clasps her hands together
to pray? She lashes her fingers
fingertip to knuckle
fingertip to knuckle
fingertip to knuckle
thumbs forward and crossed.

In this way she plays out
the rituals of her childhood—
ablutions and prayers before bed
followed by hours
of tossing and turning,
twisting through the night
like a leaf caught up in the wind.

A cup of sky before bed—
the scent of stars—a bowl of sleep
heavy in her hands.

What Poets Do
for Marie Howe and Jorie Graham

As the poet reads, all I can see,
focus on, are her large hands,
her fingers slender and splayed
against the black curtain,
the velvet backdrop.
They move, open, close,
like a bird that can't decide
where to come to rest.
They reach out—the right hand
directing the poem as she reads,
the palm pale, her fingers flushed,
rose-red.

Another reading, years ago,
I became fixated on the poet's hair,
long thick spiral curls bouncing
as she flung it back and forth,
from side to side, shoulder
to shoulder simultaneously flipping
a long-fringed scarf across her neck
like a whip, guillotining her words
as they escaped from her mouth.

I've Lost the Language

I've lost the language I need to speak with you.
My tongue stutters across the continents of your name,
                burrows
when it sees the clear bowl of vowels that have gathered
there. I've lost the language I need to call you to mind.
My eyes are blind
                to your reflection in the mirror.
I wait for you to answer while you travel my landscape,
              you are
without image, without name.
I wait for you to answer, but your mouth has filled
with mud. Your hands
                have gone to dust.
I reach out to touch the old bones of your fingers.
They break apart and topple like pick-up sticks.

Sometimes I Pray that You Won't Talk to Me

Adrienne knew the wholeness of being alone,
as a plane rides lonely and level on its radio beam.

And, I admit, there are times when I wish
that you would walk on without saying hello.

I may be at a table at Arby's, reading or staring,
and you may think that I am lonely, alone,

but I will be thinking my own thoughts
with no regard to how I look as I unwrap

my Jr. sandwich, slow-turning the pages
of the latest mystery I've been reading.

If you see me in the park, on a bench
or on a trail, know that I am not looking for you.

I will be waiting, like Mary O., for the trees
to reveal the yellow paint-splash of the warbler.

It will be dangerous to approach me, lost
as I am inside my own head. I may

mistake you for a honeybee. Or a tiger.
Conversation comes hard for the wanderer,

for the one born with silence always
clamoring for attention in our heads.

Our eyes hear more than voices,
our feet lead us away from your world.

We are not immortal, no, nor are we
more sacred, but the sacred comes to us

in our solitude, in the brush of tree bark
under our hands, in the soft way the sun

cups the star-studded Potentilla
in the fast food parking lot,

yes, even there.

Surely It Hasn't Come to This

I'd like to say that I am interested in everything
but it is just not true, not true—
the world goes to war and I am obsessed
with the news for a whole day, but then
I go to bed and all I can think of is the itch
just below my right shoulder blade—
the unreachable itch, the pull and stretch
of my left arm behind and around
my back, fingernails desperately turned
to the thing that won't leave me alone
and all night long, on certain dedicated
channels, the newsreels bomb
the living shit out of Syrians, and
dissenting Pakistanis build bombs
and Kurds and Turks continue to insist
that they are more different than alike
and my arm snakes behind me
like a traitor, and all through the night
the president-elect tweets his sad
complaints and I am better than this
or no better, not true, it is just
not true that everything I am interested in
is more than what I say, than what I feel,
in the long night of the insistent
itch.

Mitosis

Overnight, some essential part of her
shifted, pulled away—feverish
and buzzing like a failing
fluorescent light.

She felt the tug of it
in her head and her chest,
the moment of separation
echoing.

By morning it had settled
into a small pulsing moon
that orbited her mother-body,
a wan amber glow.

Finally, it stopped circling
and rested, like a house light
just outside the door
of her belly.

This is the embryo of my
next life, she thought, as it
thrummed and flickered,
separate from her now

but close enough
to reach
with extended hand, to
caress it

or fling it away,
this embryonic life
in waiting, the old death
sloughing away.

Desire, At Sixty

Whatever it is, if it is not water
it should be the opposite of water.
It should spark and snap.
It should crackle with static electricity
when you try to pick it up.
Whatever it is, if it is not water
it should be merciless
as thorns, as burs, as
gravel on a fallen knee.
Whatever it is, if it does not move
like water—languid as a snake
in the sun—then it should be
solid, indefatigable, permafrost.
If it is not love that wraps its
liquid arms around you
and pulls you down,
then—whatever it is—it must,
at least, be fierce.

www.ingramcontent.com/pod-product-compliance
Lightning Source LLC
LaVergne TN
LVHW041553070426
835507LV00011B/1067